What People are Saying . . .

"Very entertaining story of one man's conflict between profit-motive production forestry and his underlying desire to protect and wisely use the forest resource. Once you begin reading, you won't be able to put it down."

"The Indian flavor in the book could lead to rituals in the practical *deed* side for people wanting to become a Rainbow Warrior. Motivating and thought provoking. Students would appreciate it."

"This book reflects the growing concern about how we use our forest resources. It could be used as a starting point for discussion of the forest management issues facing this nation."

"To save wildlife, plants and animals, we must conserve whole ecosystems and habitats. *Call of the Rainbow Warrior* stimulates this awareness through a wonderfully moving fable, then provides action and opportunity through an excellent, annotated bibliography which alone is worth the price of the book. *Warrior* convinces all ages to take responsibility—we are all caretakers of our Earth."

CALL OF THE RAINBOW WARRIOR

An Environmental Fable

Twyla Dell

FORE SIGHT INSTITUTE
Overland Park, KS

ISBN 0-9626197-0-1
LCCN 90-081281

Rainbow Warrior design by Gavin Dell.

Dedication

To my sons, Brennan and Gavin, and all the other young people who inherit this world from my generation and whose task it will be to make it habitable for those who follow.

Buy a Book
Help Plant a Tree

We believe in returning to the Earth what we take from it. Since it takes trees to create books, it seems fair to replenish the tree population from which paper comes. We also believe in blooming where we are planted. Because we live, work and play in the heartland of America, we at The Foresight Institute has arranged with the State and Extension Forestry, Kansas State University, to help plant a tree for each copy sold of *Call of the Rainbow Warrior.*

We acknowledge you for your support in helping us replenish nature's storehouse and for your part in reforesting America. You'll see your trees planted along highways, on median strips and in the communities of Kansas.

We invite every publishing company in America to do the same.

Contents

Foreword

When I was a young child, we lived on a farm in Oregon a few miles south of Salem. It was a small farm, typical in those days. I walked a mile on graveled roads to a two-room schoolhouse containing all eight elementary grades.

We had a small stand of fir trees at the rear of our acreage in which I loved to play. I took my dolls and sat among the thick ferns on moss-covered logs and played make believe. It was a beautiful spot, the kind Laura Ingalls Wilder of *Little House on the Prairie* would have treasured. I shared that place with all kinds of wild creatures from snakes and salamanders to birds, foxes, raccoons, possums and more, but never with another playmate. Alone there, I could see and hear things that seemed to disappear when someone else came with me.

One night at the dinner table my family discussed the fact that the trees on the adjoining land had been sold for timber. I couldn't fathom what that meant. The next time I played in my hideout, I could hear the distant drone of trucks and bulldozers. As the days went by that sound grew louder and louder. One summer afternoon I heard voices so close I ran along the nearly invisible path to our property line. Loggers, marking the trees for cutting, walked the line and called to each other. With sudden, ferocious courage

I stepped from the woods to the fence and said, gesturing to our stand, "These trees our ours and you can't have them!"

Two men turned to locate the sound of that little voice. As they saw me standing pint-sized against the trees, they laughed. I bolted into the woods. I never told my folks about that encounter, but listened to their discussion each night with growing dread of this threat to our place.

Finally, the day came when all five of us stood at our strand of barbed wire and watched them log to within an inch of our property line. We watched as the hillside beyond us was cleared of every tree of any size and the ground was churned into lifeless mush. Such a loss of nature was beyond my understanding.

From then on I entered my little hideaway turned sanctuary with different feelings. It wasn't just *there* as it had been, it was now to be protected as precious and sacred. Sometimes I would walk the final distance to our fence to survey that denuded hillside and watch for signs of returning life. That sight was my somber awakening to man's ability to strike dead something I couldn't conceive of losing.

At the dinner table the logging dominated our conversation for months. We vowed that no matter how tough our lives became, we'd *never* sell our trees. And we never did. When we left the farm—on which we could not make a living—a few years later our small stand of trees pierced the horizon like a sentinel. I secretly believed I had sole responsibility for their survival.

I didn't return to that spot for more than twenty years. When I finally did, my trees were gone. I was struck with heart-wrenching guilt. I hadn't been there to protect them.

To this day I don't know how to do that, but this book is my best effort.

Part I

Call of the
Rainbow Warrior

Richard Lawless paused at the door of his factory and surveyed it with both eagerness and frustration. The early morning light filled a patch of floor at his feet as he stepped over the threshold. He always arrived an hour before the machines started up.

The timber industry had been good to him. He had started as a management trainee twenty-five years ago. He'd learned quickly, become vice-president and then gone out on his own. Now he was chief executive officer of his own plant.

He took a deep breath of fresh-cut wood. Like the scent of a beautiful woman, that fragrance never failed to intoxicate him. He paused at the door every morning to fill his lungs with the sweet smell of success. He loved this place. Always had—and for that matter always would. This factory was him—an extension of his flesh in the form of machinery, equipment, people and paper. He and the business were closer than he and his wife, his kids, his parents, even his brother Phil—Rich's shadow in his growing-up years.

Rich had built this business from scratch eighteen years ago when the trees were thick around the small cabins and uncurbed main street of this frontier town. He loved coming to work here every day. It was his play, his fun. In a great rush of focused passion he had splashed the seed of his vision against the womb of the universe and created this new entity. What fun it had been to wheel and deal in setting it up, to demand from the world supplies, parts, people and customers, to face the impossible and make it happen, to sweat out the agony of meeting payroll and raising capital.

He had never had that much fun since. Ever. Anywhere. Not in all the civic offices he had held, not in the trips to Europe and the board meetings with big-time business personalities. Nothing compared to the calculated risk, the stretch of the sinews of his mind and body, the sweat of total concentration toward this success. That was bliss. That was life at its best.

The years since had been a slow descent from that orgasmic high. Risks had been fewer, challenges smaller and details of maintenance and growth piled higher. And government regulations. They were the worst part—pollution regulations. Those were the source of his frustration. The Environmental Protection Agency was on his back, had been for over fifteen years. That bunch of bureaucrats, more than any single factor, had taken the fun out of his business. Now he was facing an eco-terrorist group in court who were trying to stop his operation. Friday was the showdown. That didn't worry him. Let them sue; he was ready. He'd sue them back for interrupting his operation. A $25,000 fine ought to cool their heels and keep them out of his hair. This was war!

He had learned to survive the hard way, through years of business' giddy highs and breathtaking lows. He would survive and beat them. He would watch them eat their regulations, their *planet-before-people* junk. He would. . . .

He stopped in his tracks, his thought unfinished. A rainbow descended from one of the high windows and fell across the floor, bathing machinery and equipment in a shower of color that changed them from utilitarian drab to pieces of art in colored light and shadow. How odd. How . . . unearthly. Richard cocked his head and eyed it warily, half suspicious, half enjoying the transformation. How could a rainbow do that?

Then he heard music playing somewhere far away, a haunting woodwind pipe of some kind. The sound of that pipe in the silent building touched him. It was so plaintive, beseeching, evocative. Where was it coming from? Then the telephone rang and Richard Lawless jumped; he ran to pick it up.

By the time he had taken care of a dozen crises, demands and opportunities the day had waned and he had forgotten the rainbow. That was the stuff of business, Rich thought as he propped his feet on his desk and relaxed for a well-earned rest. The clock said 2:25. He had been here since 6 o'clock and would put another four or five hours in before he left. He breathed deeply of a cigarette and thought wryly that was exactly why he was now a free man and not a functioning husband and father. Too much time given to the mistress of his life. Marilyn was a good woman, too. A good wife and mother. He had no quarrel with her. Nor she with him. As she said, he was just married to someone else.

Ruth, his secretary, interrupted his musings. "Rich, your brother is on the line again. I told him you were busy."

Rich shook his head. "What has gotten into him? Is there no peace? No 'no' for an answer?"

A mental picture of Phil and himself as kids passed through his mind. They had been so close. Such a pair of *polliwogs* as their mother called them. Phil so softhearted and sensitive and Rich so daring and tough.

And now they were on opposite sides of the issue that would spell prosperity or doom for his company.

He nodded at Ruth and picked up the phone. "Hey, bro, what's up?" In spite of their differences, he couldn't be unkind to Phil.

"Rich!" Phil answered. "Now don't hang up until you've heard me out. I have a video I'd like you to see. It's about twenty minutes long. It will really help you understand what we're talking about—the difference between short-term and long-term thinking. I'd like to come by in a few minutes and show it to you. Are you available for about a half an hour?"

Rich did not reply. *"Phil, be my old bro again. Just drop this tiresome cause of saving the trees. You can't save trees. They're a commodity, like cotton and sheep. They're not meant to be saved."*

Phil went on. "As you know, we'll be seeing you at the hearing on Friday. All our people have seen the video. I thought you'd like to as well."

"Phil, you're trying to kill my business. You think I'll kill her for your sake? You want me to let all my people go? You keep your trees pristine and unlogged and I'll close up my plant and put everyone out of work?"

He glanced at his calendar. "Phil," he said, "it so happens I'm giving the graduation speech at the high school Thursday night and between that and the court case, I'm busy preparing."

"It's only about twenty minutes, Rich. I'll be in and out in half an hour," Phil offered.

"Just what do you hope to gain from showing me this video?"

"I want you to see what kind of a world we're leaving our children if we don't stop throwing away our natural resources with no thought of tomorrow."

Rich took his feet off the desk and hunched over the phone. "That's a cheap shot and you know it.

There's nothing wrong with this world and there's nothing wrong with the way we use your sacred natural resources. What we do has worked for two hundred years and it will continue to work.

"As for our kids, they already have it too easy. Look, you know it's not going to change my mind. Forget it. You can't have it two ways. I'm not giving up my business to satisfy your demands."

"Rich, you keep accusing me of *either-or* thinking. I'm not suggesting that. What we need is a new definition of business success that *includes* the environment. We can't just keep cutting and selling every log to Japan, China and Korea while our own mills are shutting down for lack of work. It's not just how much we're cutting, it's how we're using what we cut, and what we're leaving behind. And how long do you think this area can tolerate your *accelerated harvest* notion? You know you're not replanting at the pace you're clear cutting. Events are demanding a change, and rather than fighting them, you're in a perfect position to lead them."

"Phil, you've told me this before. It's getting on my nerves and so, unfortunately, are you. I don't want to be rude, but I'm really very busy. I'll see you on Friday." Rich replaced the phone quickly. Such treatment of his brother pained him, but business was business. He had to return a dividend to his stockholders or he was in deep trouble. He had to meet the payments on the debt he'd acquired by expanding and investing in new properties. Having just met with the board two days before, their message was fresh in his mind.

"Rich?" Jerry, his floor supervisor, was at the door. "Sylvia Field was late again today. I'm trying to work with her, but you said rules are rules. What do you want me to do?"

"She still hasn't found a babysitter? It can't be that hard to find someone to take care of kids. Where are all the women these days?"

"She and a couple of others have proposed to open a nursery and day care center here at the plant," Jerry said. Jerry's hopeful tone indicated he plainly thought the idea had worth.

Rich shot out of his chair. "Now that is an absurd notion. No way. They'd be off looking after those kids every time they cried. If they can't handle the problem that's their tough luck. I understand K-Mart hires part time."

"She's a good worker," Jerry said. "I hate to lose her over this."

"She's not so good we can't find someone to replace her. This plant has grown because we kept our mind on business and didn't mix it with anything else," he said almost savagely.

"OK, boss," Jerry said, leaning away from this verbal onslaught. He hesitated a moment as if wanting to argue the question.

"Well?" Rich asked brusquely.

Jerry looked down at his boots and shrugged. "Whatever you say." He closed the door and left Rich to sink into his chair.

By 4:30 the pace was slowing. Rich was replacing the phone from the twenty-second call of the day when he heard women's voices arguing in the outer office.

He looked up to see Sylvia Field standing in the doorway, her face tight with anger. She had stepped past Ruth who was attempting to block her way. Sylvia was a tall, willowy woman—in her early thirties, he judged. She had worked in a technical capacity with Jerry for about nine months. Her references had been good. Her work was good. She was bright and willing and full of ideas, but her attendance problem was wearying.

"You're firing me because I can't find a babysitter?" she demanded hotly. "Do you have any idea how difficult it is to be a single mother and constantly be torn between your children and your job? I'm a good worker. I like my job. I need your help. Firing me won't fix my problem or yours."

Rich, a little taken aback by such directness, said, "Sylvia. Come in and sit down." He closed the door behind her. "Jerry tells me you've been late a number of times. You know our rule here about being at your workstation on time."

"I know that. I've done my best to be here. But the shortage of child care in this town is unbelievable. I can't leave my son with just any warm body. He's only three and a half. My daughter is eight. She isn't old enough to be left home alone with him. There are several of us here in the same position. Why can't we use that spare storage room for a child-care center. We could fix it up and hire someone. . . ."

Rich interrupted her. "I know that seems a perfectly reasonable solution to you but it's not an option from my point of view. We're not in the child-care business. We're in the timber business. We're here to make a profit for the stockholders and that's what we're doing."

His voice rose again and he forcibly lowered it to a more conciliatory tone. "We do appreciate your good work and your interest in doing more of it. But when you were hired you knew the rules. You told us you could comply with those rules. We've done our part. We're sorry to lose you. You have been a good worker, and we'll be glad to recommend your work—apart from your attendance problem—to another employer. I wish we could accommodate your needs. But if we met your demands we'd have to meet everyone's and that's not what business is about." He straightened up feeling that he had made his point rather grandly.

Sylvia gave him a poisonous look. "Mr. Lawless, with all due respect for your success here, you don't have a clue to what business is about. Business is about serving the community from which it draws its life, not ignoring it. It's about creating successful situations for your employees, not about discarding them when they don't fit your neat little rules."

Rich sat transfixed by such gall. Before he could respond, she plunged ahead, nearly jabbing his chest with her finger as she worked herself into the depths of her argument.

"You know those Planet-Before-People folks who scream at us at the front gate to stop destroying their ecosystem? Well, I'm part of *your* ecosystem. Maybe it's time to take care of both of us." She turned and stomped out of the office.

After that he drowned himself in paperwork. He refused to think about Sylvia. He would not be sucked into social work for the sake of a few women who wanted the business world to treat them in a special way. He found most of these so-called crises were simply nuisances. If you ignored disgruntled employees long enough they finally went away. And if they didn't, you dealt with them. As for the hearing? He left that to his lawyers.

He entered his silent condominium at 7 o'clock that night. The absence of his family still struck a hollow note for a moment as he closed the door behind him. Even though he had always left home early and returned late, someone had been there to appreciate the number of dragons he had slain for them that day, as he used to say. He knew, of course, that he had done it because he loved doing it. They probably knew it too, but always acknowledged his stories of business Derring-do with enthusiastic interest. Now there were no kisses, no chit chat. Just him and four walls.

He had given Marilyn the house. Their kids were in high school and he didn't want to disrupt their lives. In fact, his daughter Kim would be in the graduating class he was addressing on Thursday. Quickly, he sorted the mail. Ah, there were the tickets for Cancún. Good. As soon as the hearing with the eco-freaks was over, he and the kids were taking off.

He tore the cardboard from a microwave dinner and nuked it while he poured himself a beer. As he stared dully at the empty room, his eyes rested on the graduation picture of Kim. She was a beauty, like her mother. And another photo of their son Dan, also like his mother. Didn't he get any credit? Well, he had the business.

He pulled some handwritten sheets over to him—his speech for Thursday. He had written a good portion of it already. It was full of mottos of his success. All the old-fashioned stuff that had gotten him where he was: Hard work pays off! So what if it was a nose-to-the-grindstone kind of speech? That's what had made this country great—his company great. As a formula for success, it was hard to beat hard work and concentration, by God, and he wanted to make sure those over-indulged kids understood the American work ethic before they got too soft in their ways. If he, the local hero, said it, maybe it would carry some weight.

An hour of television and a quick bath and Richard Lawless sank gratefully into his bed. He tossed and turned. Echoes of Phil and Sylvia played through his mind. He tried to concentrate on Cancún. That was a restful spot. Finally he slept.

Part II

At first he thought nothing of the stone steps rising under his feet. He had trod them all his life. He raised his fine robe to make sure his sandaled feet fit well on the narrow riser and then the next and the next. He raised a hand to check his heavy headdress. It was secure.

Usually he exulted in this climb, but today his heart was heavy with sorrow. As high priest of the sacred city of Chichén Itzá, he was about to perform an awesome task that came just once a year. He was dedicating the lives of the prince and princess to the Feathered Serpent before they were sacrificed. These two young people were to be thrown ceremoniously into the sacred well at the end of the short road from the pyramid. For a year they had been tenderly cared for, given anything they wanted and offered every choice privilege and prize. But now they must pay the price. And the price this year was no less than the salvation of the entire city.

He stopped half way up the great pyramid and gazed out over the grandeur of the city, hewn out of white limestone and painted with murals of warriors, skulls, gods. How handsome it was. How much a part of him it was. He watched the sun rising over the observatory in the distance. He saw the ceremonial ball court off to his left and the temple of the skulls on the road to the sacred well.

He felt tears prick his eyes at the beauty of this familiar scene. What a loss. What a loss. The entire place would soon be deserted forever. They had to leave—every last one of them. The fields had died around the city. For the sixth growing season the fields had failed to produce enough for them to eat. Within a day's walk from the city all the trees had been cut down. And new growth failed to appear soon enough to feed and warm his people. He recalled an old woman approaching him on the road. "The land is tired," she had told him. "It can bear no more children."

He continued his climb now acutely aware that this was his very last trip up the sacred steps that only he and a few other priests were allowed to touch. He, the chief priest, had prayed more and more fervently as the days had turned into seasons. He had sacrificed more and more until the stone table at the top of the Temple of the Warriors had turned as black with dried blood as his obsidian knife. Nothing had worked. It was clear his people could no longer grow enough crops to support themselves. The torrential rains had washed away the remaining soil. Now great gullies ran through once fertile fields and the rivers turned to mud when it rained.

His last climb. He would lose this vantage point. He would be forever on a level with the commoners. They would see him as ordinary. His days of high priesthood were over.

Pressing tightly together at the base of the pyramid, the people murmured prayers as he stepped to the ground. The prince and princess were brought in on their platforms, their hands and feet bound with golden chains. He lifted his voice to the gods. The soft guttural sounds of the language filled the air as he chanted the sacred verses over and over.

"Please, dear beautiful, bountiful one. Please restore the earth to us. Please fill our fields once more with glorious crops as before. Please give us trees for wood again. What have we done to deserve your wrath? Why do you turn from us in our time of need?"

A woodwind played along with him from somewhere, sweetly lilting and haunting. It had such a tender, hopeful quality, that he paused from his abstracted state to see where it was coming from. Were the heavens offering him a sign at last? He glanced over the crowds. Did they hear it? He couldn't identify a musician among them.

His assistants and he worked automatically together for one last time. The ceremony went on with the people's reply. It rumbled up from them, bouncing off the stone steps. Gathered for this final, total plea for help, they sounded sad, angry, frightened.

He descended the steps reluctantly, giving up each one with personal regret. Here was the chipped step. Here was the green-flecked one. At this point he could barely see the tip of the observatory. He knew each step by heart.

The crowd parted for him at the bottom of the stairs. More than sad, they seemed angry. At him. They muttered and shook their fists. What had he done? Why were they angry at him?

Hadn't he prayed with every element of his body for their salvation? He moved to the head of the procession and led the way toward the sacred well. The prince and princess sat silently on their platforms. The woodwind, now strengthened with drums, grew louder and took on the cadence of a march. The crowd stepped in time to it. They passed the temple of the skulls. Human skulls carved on each limestone block of the temple witnessed the procession as it rounded the bend in the road.

At that moment a strange sigh washed over the crowd. He looked up to see a brilliant rainbow in the sky ending beyond the well. Perhaps the heavens had opened and pointed bright-colored fingers at their place of travail. He, too, said, "Aah." This must be the sign he had prayed for. Praise the gods, perhaps they were saved! The woodwind sang and the drums beat faster and faster. The crowds were clapping their hands and chanting.

They reached the platform over the well. He didn't know how deep the well was. Only the dead knew. He had walked around this hole in the jungle floor once, though, and counted his steps—more than five hundred before he reached the platform again. If it was as deep as it was wide. . . . That made it very deep indeed.

The prince and princess were placed on the platform, their slender, bronze bodies wreathed in golden chains. In unison, they turned to look at him, unspeakable anguish in their eyes. Their faces stunned him. My God! They were his own children, Danny and Kim. He was paralyzed at the sight. His knees went weak. Before he could move, could reach out to stop them, with a great shout from the crowd, his two assistant priests pushed the young people over the side. He stared immovable as their bodies fell. A horrified cry ripped from his throat.

Without a word the two priests turned to him. He looked at them stricken. The one on his left was his brother Phil. He looked at the other. It was Sylvia Field. Together, grimacing in a mirthless laugh, they moved in front of him. He stepped back as they pushed him. He heard the crowd give a mighty yell of approval as he hit the side of the limestone wall and fell toward the water. . . .

* * * * *

Richard sat straight up in bed, gasping and thrashing like a drowning man. It took a moment for the scene to fade from his mind, and at last the bedroom came into focus. He searched the dim outlines of the room for the familiar shapes of furniture. He was in his own bed. That horror had been a dream. Why should he dream something so terrifying?

He rose and went to the bathroom. Then, too shaken to return to bed, he padded into the living room and looked again at the two photos of his children. He loved those kids. Why would he dream anything so crazy? What had he eaten that had so colored his subconscious mind? He sat in the easy chair near their photos and drank in the sight of their smiles until—at last—he quieted himself and dozed.

*   *   *   *   *

The next day at work Richard found himself a little edgy. He jumped at slight noises and rasped out orders to Ruth. He wanted to share his dream with someone. But who? He recognized part of the free-man syndrome. If you wake up alone you have no one to share with.

He dodged the telephone and worked on his speech, glanced through the latest reports from various departments—in general, forced himself to become engrossed in his work. In reality, he was keeping his head below the line of fire. Yesterday and last night had been a bit much.

Speaking of yesterday, he thought, don't I hear Phil's voice again? He groaned and looked up.

Phil brushed past Ruth and into the office. He had a slighter build than Richard's but otherwise looked like he'd hatched from the same brood. He was carrying a video tape.

"Hi, Rich," he said breezily. "You remember what Mom always said when she wanted to make us do something we didn't want to? 'You'll be glad you did afterwards. It's much easier than you think.' Remember that? I just had to show you this tape." He proceeded straight to the bookcase and inserted the cartridge in

Rich's VCR. He kept his back to his brother behind the desk.

Rich felt a rush of emotion at such highhandedness. Beneath all this current squabble, he loved Phil. He admired him for not taking no for an answer and for waltzing in and ignoring his wishes. It was a gesture worthy of himself in his buccaneering days. But he was also totally offended at being outmaneuvered and forced to give in—on his own territory! Especially on a day when he still bore in his throat the dark-brown taste of the nightmare.

"Phil," he said, trying to sound casual, "you're one heck of a brother. If I didn't love you, I'd kill you on the spot." It suddenly occurred to him he could tell Phil his dream. He would love it. He was in it, after all. They used to whisper together in bed as kids and tell each other nauseous ghost jokes and ghastly fantasies that only pubescent boys exchange with bosom buddies.

But Phil was on another track. "Rich, this is a tape about the rain forest destruction in Brazil. The Northwest isn't the only place where wholesale forest destruction is going on. I thought if you saw this you'd understand more about what's happening right here."

Rich's eyes bulged at such a statement.

Phil rushed on. "It was just shot last month by some scientists working there to protect the wildlife. The implications of it are frightening for us all. You'll never think of trees the same after you see this. Trees are not just board feet of lumber!" He smiled nervously at Richard, pushed the tape in and punched the button.

Instantly the room was filled with the sound of bulldozers and chain saws. A great, wrenching crack of a giant tree leaving its stump and crashing to the ground made Rich wince. A man's voice narrated somewhat breathlessly, as if he'd been running, that the great forests of Brazil were being desecrated at the appalling rate of one football-field-sized area per second. The pressure and trauma on the wildlife and plant life was beyond measure, the voice said huskily. Species were becoming extinct at a rate faster than any time since the dinosaurs disappeared. Whole species of plants and animals were being obliterated before their existence had been observed and catalogued. The rain forest had been a treasure house of medical beginnings. And now, miracle medicines were being lost before they were found.

Scenes of blackened, smoking spires and withering crops on cleared lands came next, then droves of long-horned cattle clipping sparse grassland. The camera zeroed in on a small monkey clinging furtively to a tree limb. Its simian face was frozen in fear. Beyond it, other forest creatures leaped through the fires as men hacked vines with their machetes and chain saws. Brown-toothed, red-eyed refugees from the city grinned at the cameras as they tore at their country's backlands for a spot to call their own. Rich shuddered in spite of himself. I am witnessing a glimpse of Armageddon, he thought.

Then anger rose. He knew all this stuff. So what was the backdrop of actual footage supposed to lend to these statistics? He hated this heartstring approach to winning him over. What did Brazil have to do with *him*? He didn't harvest Brazilian lumber.

He lunged out of his chair and turned the tape off. Phil stepped back, tensed for an attack. With great effort Rich brought himself under control. Phil was doing what he thought best. Rich had been at least this obnoxious himself when he pursued his own goals.

"Phil," he said evenly with a crooked smile on his face, "thanks for coming by." He punched the eject button on the VCR and handed Phil the tape, put his hand on Phil's shoulder and propelled him toward the door.

"See you on Friday. You coming to Kim's graduation? Great. Then I'll see you Thursday night." He pushed Phil through the door and closed it quietly behind him.

He must buy Ruth a football uniform, he thought, or else hire a bouncer. This was becoming ridiculous.

* * * * *

Rich spent the evening working on his speech for the commencement ceremony. He took the event seriously—not just because his daughter was graduating with this class. In May he had been named Businessman of the Year for the state, an honor of which he felt quite proud. The award had been a high spot in a career sloping toward the downhill. With Marilyn gone, the leveraged buy-out, the heavy debt, the pressure from the Japanese, as well as the EPA regulations and the eco-freaks wearing away at him, the honor had rejuvenated him.

He saw the speech as an opportunity not only to enhance his image as a business leader but to forge a closer bond with Kim as well. She was special and this was her special day. He would be there for her in a way that none of the other fathers would be. He would make Kim proud of him. He could imagine the other kids rolling their eyes and pointing at him on the stage and teasing Kim. She'd pretend to be mortified but, in fact, would love every minute of it.

Close to 11:00 he crept reluctantly into bed. Just the sight of the sheets recalled that bloodcurdling scene at the edge of the sacred well in Chichén Itzá. He shrugged off the memory and wished himself a better

night. The emotional load of the last two days over-
came him and he slept.

* * * * *

He awoke to the sound of swishing leaves and
smooching noises behind him. He rolled over in the
crook of the tree and looked. His fellows frolicked
about in the tree limbs, reaching out their long, red-
dish-brown, hairy arms to each other. They clasped the
bald red heads of their mates to their breasts and
kissed each other with agile lips. They chattered,
purred and chirped to each other.

He loved that sound. It meant warm bodies and full
stomachs and safe places to play and dance. He heard
the yowl of a big cat far off. An anaconda slithered by
overhead and a giant anteater shuffled slowly past
below. He reached up and patted the lush vegetation
over his head. The fur that lined his upper arms
brushed his face.

Such leaves. Such flowers. Yellow, pink with white
centers, long tongues of orange. Beautiful. A macaw
squawked and flew away, brilliant feathers catching a
shaft of sun. He looked for the sky through the thick
leaves but the dense canopy overhead all but blocked
it out.

He reached over to his mate. Her red-brown hair
caught a bit of sunlight. Her perfect little red face and
slanted brown eyes returned his look. She was beautiful, too. Encircled in her long hairy arms, she suckled
a tiny infant clinging to her breast. It was new. Her
dark eyes were half shut with contentment. They were
safe here, he thought. No more running from fire and
men-kill. He stretched and yawned.

In the distance he could hear a tender melody, soulful, graceful, caressing. Ah! Rest here, peace here, it said. The whole forest seemed to take notice. Slowly the mood of the forest quickened. The pace of the music grew faster. He sat up and grunted, touching his mate with a leathery brown finger. She also stood up.

In the small clearing ahead of them, animals began to congregate. The music gyrated like whirling leaves after a gust of wind. Good. Once before, this had happened. He remembered it with joy. When he was young and his mother still held him this had happened. He nodded; his bald red head bounced up and down. His face relaxed. His short, fat tail wiggled. Fun. He smooched his mate. She chirped and smooched him back.

The air trembled with vibrations of the myriad life forms dancing to the music. The trees swayed. Their very trunks seemed to vibrate; their branches strummed in time to the music. A thrill of power filled the air. He could feel the hairs rising on the back of his neck to the joy of the frolicking pack. The flowers seemed to lift their blossoms and move to the music. The forest celebrated itself.

Such pounding joy, such fever, such juicy good fun. He flung back his head and crowed, pounding his small muscled chest. Good. Fun.

The tempo shifted and the whole of the scene seemed suffused with different colored lights. Red, blue, green, yellow, orange. The colors swirled in time to the music.

He laughed a hollow, coughing laugh and wriggled his buttocks. His tail shot out behind him like an arrow. He stamped his feet. His blood sang, his fists pumped the air. He nodded at his mate. She too gyrated with the irresistible rhythm. The music rose to crescendo. Ooooh.

Then a great cracking sound overtook their ecstasy. Something screamed. He stopped in his tracks. He smelled smoke. For an instant there was stillness. Then the rainbow colors seemed to shatter and cascade to the forest floor. He heard their tinkling as they fell to the ground. The music faded.

He heard the roar of that great yellow jaw that pushed over trees. He heard the voices of men-kill. They carried a screaming, churning thing in their hands that sliced through their tree as if it were a ripe banana. He reached for his mate. His fellows screeched and chattered, scattering to higher limbs. Some flung themselves to other trees as the solid perch they knew so well shuddered and jerked in its death throes. They hurled hate and fear at the men-kill with every scream.

The cracking sound of the falling tree drowned all other noise. He and his mate rode it to the ground. She flew from his grasp on impact, crashing into the underbrush ahead. He lunged to free himself from the wreckage of the tree. He was caught. A white-hot pain shot through his body. Men-kill ran to the spot where his mate fell. Searched with clumsy, heavy feet for his mate and infant. He willed himself to run to her, but his breath came only in wisps and gasps. He twisted to see men-kill come out of the underbrush. They laughed and shook their fists and held up his mate. She lived! Miraculously, the child clung to her. They looked so tiny and so far away. Then men-kill threw a net over his screaming mate and their child and slung it on his back.

He could not move. She screamed for his help. Her thin arm stretched through the net, searched the air for something to grab onto. He tried to reach out to her. He could not move his once strong body. Only his eyes helped her go before the blackness came.

* * * * *

Rich felt for the bed, grabbed the sheets on either side of him and twisted them into wads with his fists. What *in the world* was going on?

He forbade himself to move until his breathing slowed and his eyes opened on their own. Again the familiar bedroom greeted his hesitant look. He let out his breath and sat up. His back didn't hurt. He could move. Oh, that was the dream. It had been so real. Just like the previous night. How could he dream like that two nights in a row? Was his food laced with acid?

He shook off the terror of that last scene as his mate had screamed for deliverance from the men-kill.

He could wring Phil's neck for bringing over that sensationalist video and stuffing it down his throat. It was like a Vietnam war movie, calculated to leave you sunk in your chair, eyes filled with tears at the senseless loss, the confusion of values, your guts ripped to shreds at man's stupidity.

He sat up the rest of the night and smoked and wondered what was coming next and what he would do when it came.

* * * * *

Of all days, he had a tour of sixth graders through the plant. What timing. He knew from the way the anger came unbidden with every thought that he was strung out. He'd have to be careful or he'd bite some kid's head off. The teachers would look wounded and disappointed, the little brat would cry, and twenty years worth of breaking his back for this community would go up in smoke.

Usually he enjoyed showing up for these groups. Their eyes were full of awe, their questions memorable and surprising. Like the kid who had asked, "Mr. Lawless, where do trees go when they die?"

Rich had smiled. "Why, they come here, of course. That's what the timber business is about."

"No," the child persisted. "Do they go to heaven?"

He had chuckled then. Darned if he knew. Darned if he'd ever thought of it. "Oh. I'm sure they do. I'm sure trees have souls just as you and I do." He had raised his eyebrows quizzically. Had that answered? Yes? Good.

But today his nerves were shredded. He wanted to hide out in his office. He seemed to be doing a lot of that lately. It was *his* company. What was going on? He asked himself that question for the hundredth time that week.

The telephone rang. It was the reference librarian. He had called to find out what kind of animal he had been in his dream. He couldn't remember seeing anything exactly like it.

"A red uakari," he repeated as he wrote it down. "And that's a New-World ape, you say."

"Yes, from the family Cebidae." the librarian continued. "I'm sure from your description that's what it was. Red-brown coat and vermillion face. Odd looking things, aren't they? The uakari grows to about 50-60 centimeters—that's about 20-24 inches—as an adult. Weighs about 5 kilos—about 11-12 pounds. They're the only New-World monkey with a short tail, only about 6 inches long. They're a great black-market prize. Hotly traded for zoos and animal collectors. They're an endangered species, of course. In fact, now extremely rare. You see, they don't last long in captivity, it says here. Some effort is being made to protect them and restore them to their natural habitat but with all the clearing of the rain forest. . . ."

"Yes, I know. Thank you," Richard interrupted. "Thank you very much. You've been most helpful," he hastened to add in a pleasing tone in case he had been too abrupt. He didn't want the librarian carrying tales. But . . . he couldn't handle another syllable about rain forests.

His secretary rang. The sixth graders were outside. And sure enough, the kids were in great shape today. He felt vulnerable though, almost nervous. *Did* trees have souls, he wondered? They had almost seemed to in his dream.

"So, that's what we do here at RJL International," he said, finishing his brief homily. Ruth handed each child a brochure explaining the process, a brief history of the business and Richard Lawless' place as founder of it.

"Mr. Lawless," one child asked. "What about all the trees you're cutting faster and faster?

For a split second Richard wanted to turn and walk away, but he took a breath, smiled instead and said, "I'm pleased to be able to tell you that this company has always stayed within federal regulations. It's part of our long-term commitment to the environment. *Geez, I'm sounding like Phil.* We work closely with the U. S. Forest Service," he finished.

"But, isn't your company being sued by the "Planet Peop . . . Planet Before People," asked another child twisting through the words.

Richard glanced at the teacher. She was squelching a smile. She'd put them up to this, had encouraged them to nail him to the wall on his own ground!

"It's true we're attending a hearing with those folks on Friday. But it isn't adversarial. We're in compliance, as they say, and the public is invited to come and see that indeed we are. It's something we do as part of protecting the public good, and we're glad to be able to participate. *"Good grief, Dickie, you should be a politician. You're as good as they are at 'double-speaking'."*

The smile had left the teacher's face. *"Well, what do you want? A confession?"*

Ruth appeared at the door. "An urgent call for you, Mr. Lawless," she said. *"Thank you, Ruth! Remind me to give you a raise."*

"Thanks for coming, boys and girls." He nodded at the teacher, smiling broadly and keeping her eye. He refused to look guilty for her satisfaction.

And so the day passed. He did not go home that night. He couldn't face the possibility of another night like the previous two. He'd have the place fumigated and the refrigerator disinfected before he'd go through another night like those. When the divorce was in process, he had spent a few nights on a pull-out couch in a small meeting room down the hall from his suite of offices. He could use it again.

He spent the evening at his desk putting the finishing touches on his speech. He was fond of a quote by Calvin Coolidge. He wasn't sure why—except his father had quoted it like gospel—so he closed with, "The business of America is business. Go forth." He glanced at the clock. It was 10:30.

He straightened the papers and counted them. Fifteen pages. A good speech. He'd have Ruth type and proof it. As he leaned back in his chair, feeling satisfied for the first time in several days, he heard that haunting woodwind again. Faintly. He stopped motionless, holding his breath, waiting to hear it continue.

There it was again. From somewhere downstairs. His skin prickled and his hair stood on end. He'd heard it now four times. Twice he'd had the life scared out of him. He stayed perfectly still and listened, trying not to let the previous terrors overcome him.

In spite of himself, he responded to the soulfulness of it. So tender, so appealing, so . . . touching. It lifted his spirits. It was so hopeful, inviting. He shook his head. No way. He wasn't going down that path again.

He rose and went out through Ruth's office into the corridor. Was it louder there? Was it in the plant where he'd seen the rainbow?

He opened the door to the plant and jumped back stunned. The music grew louder and louder while Rich stood rooted to the spot. A shaft of color swirled in front of him, shimmering, gyrating, terribly alive, pulsating with energy—all different colors at once. It was gorgeous. He thought he must be seeing the ectoplasm of a rainbow. Suddenly he was standing in it. He forgot his fear and held up his hands and turned around and around as it bathed him in its light. This ought to be in a *Star Trek* movie, he thought.

And then from the center of this intensity emerged a face . . . a being. It was . . . unspeakably beautiful, wise, stern. . . . Rich shivered as he looked into haunting eyes staring at him from behind white skin . . . no, luminescent, with rainbow colors around the eyes and chin and streaks of color on the right cheek. And rainbow hair softly floating with electric energy and piercing holes for eyes. What a face! More like a mask. He could see through it and yet it had substance and density and expression. No, Rich thought. This was more like the ending of *Close Encounters of the Third Kind.*

Rich jerked his head back slightly. It had spoken to him not so he heard it. He felt it.

Rich didn't have a clue as to what to say. Hello hardly seemed appropriate. Who was this creature? What was it? A rainbow . . . man? Person? From

somewhere came the word: Warrior. Rainbow Warrior?
Was he safe or in worse trouble than in his dreams?
He couldn't wake up from this one. He *was* awake.

A part of the rainbow reached out from the swirl of
color and took Rich's hand. Before he could reject the
offer—instantly—they were gone from the building.
Velvet blackness enveloped them. Lights twinkled here
and there. He took a deep breath and looked around.
There, against black space, hung planet Earth in its
orbit, just as in the pictures the astronauts had taken.
He looked down at his feet. His heart lurched. He was
standing in space! He jerked around, searched for the
eyes of the mask near his own face and let his breath
out slowly. His guide's serenity somehow composed
him.

Reluctantly he took his eyes off the mask and
looked at the Earth, *his* Earth again. It was so beautiful. He felt a rush of tenderness and love for this only
planet in the universe that supported the life he knew
and loved. The sight reminded him of the first time he
had seen Kim in her mother's arms. How could anything be so precious? So vulnerable? So in need of
trust and care? A tear streaked down his cheek.

He looked again into the face in the swirling rainbow and was filled with longing and tenderness, as the
music had filled him before.

Yes, he understood. It needed love and care just
like a baby. He nodded. The eyes of the mask searched
his very soul.

In a twinkling they were deep under water. Was it
the sacred well of Chichén Itzá again? No, it was the
ocean. They swam through great corral reefs that
stretched as far as his eye could see. Exquisite fish
swam past in breathtaking colors. Graceful mauve sea
anemones swayed in the currents. Over there a school
of shimmering bodies darted in and out of sunny

patches. Skulking things scuttled across the sandy bottom. It was so peaceful. It all worked so well. For a few moments they swam and watched the intricate interplay of the fish in the reef.

They moved on deeper into the ocean—a world he had never seen from the ships he'd been on. A school of large, silver bodies caught their eye and they turned to watch. Tuna! Yes, he knew that body shape. He'd fished them once. And beyond them a school of those amazing porpoises cavorting and nudging and stroking each other. He laughed as he watched them play like children.

Then a fish net fell in front of Rich and his guide and scooped up everything in its path. Everything! The abundant sea was suddenly empty. Where a heartbeat before had been teaming life, now there was nothing. He could hear the screams of the porpoises as they plunged and lunged and struggled to escape. The weight of the tuna pressed them into the nets, crushing them leaving them flapping, gasping, drowning. And where the fish had been, the sea became a desert in a matter of seconds.

He'd heard about the overfishing going on, about the reckless use of nets that gathered all in their wake, but he'd never really thought about *how much* they took.

He looked at the Rainbow Warrior's face again and shook his head.

In another twinkling he was in a small house. A half-dozen toddlers squalled and played on the floor. Sylvia Field, his former employee, languished in a tattered easy chair, watching the brood at her feet.

"Oh, now, this is too much," Rich said. "Here comes the social-work theme again. Am I responsible for her, too? I feel like Scrooge looking in on the Cratchets on Christmas Eve," he said to his companion.

A slight smile settled on the rainbow lips.

"I get it," Rich said. "Same spirit, different village idiot."

In a moment they were in a conifer forest. Ah, his trees. He was settling into sudden transitions. They walked softly on the pine needles underfoot. Rich took a deep breath of the perfumed air. He had taken the kids camping in places like this where the air was pure and silent. And the size of the trees! Huge, stately giants as old as history. At least these were safe, he thought.

The sound of a chain saw rasped almost at his side. Rich jumped away. That old, great tree he had just admired lost its home and fell, crashing into the young forest around it. When the dust settled, Richard stepped onto the cut base. It was the size of a small room. Must have been eight or ten feet across. He looked around for others like it. But he could see only young trees and scrub growth everywhere he looked— what the Forest Service liked to call the *changing resource*. It had changed, all right, from high quality to low, from big trees to broomsticks. Even Rich had to admit that.

He had just witnessed the last of the great trees falling. The others were toothpicks compared with this one. The forest had changed from here to gone, from now to nothing.

Would his grandkids ever see a tree like that, he wondered.

He looked at his companion patiently waiting near-by. The Warrior's mask shook back and forth. No.

In a twinkling he saw Kim and Dan, older—grown up, with children their age standing beside them. They looked out on acres of scrub forest, young trees, decaying stumps, clear-cut hillsides marked by gullies and mud slides, barren of life. Some areas were so pocked and lifeless they looked like lunar landscape.

"Whoa," Rich said and rubbed his eyes as if to clear them from what they had just witnessed—his children's —his grandchildren's—loss. "That's enough. I get the picture."

But his companion was relentless. Before he could say another word, they were standing on the floor of Rich's plant. At least he thought it was his plant. But it had gone to pieces if it was. The place was completely broken down. Everything was covered with layers of dust marked only by rat tracks. Ragged curtains of cobwebs let in a feeble light.

"Wait," Rich said. "This can't be my place. It's always in top-notch condition." Then he saw his company logo on the wall. "But, what happened? I'm giving it to my kids. They're who I've been working for. This is for them. In twenty years it will all be theirs."

A tattered calendar, hanging askew on the wall, marked the month of June, 2004.

"No," Rich said. He grabbed the calendar off the wall. "I know this is a dream. I get your point. I get it. I get it."

He ran around the equipment, dusting it frantically with his bare hands. "I've worked too hard for this to turn to dust. I've given it my life! Bring it back. Bring it back." He shook his fist at his companion. The face looked back, grim beyond words.

Something broke in Rich. He lunged at the figure with a mighty football tackle he hadn't used in years. His body slammed through the cloud of color into a piece of equipment.

Then the vibrating colors around it absorbed the mask. Rich leaped up as the rainbow colors swirled into a funnel cloud and rose from the factory floor creating clouds of dust. It disappeared through the roof.

"No! Don't leave me like this." Rich yelled. "Don't leave me." All the fear, loneliness and anger of the past days fell on him and he crumpled weeping, to the floor.

Part III

Richard Lawless grasped the sides of the lectern and surveyed the audience before him. He caught Kim's eye in the fifth row back on the left side. In the bleachers he saw Marilyn and Dan, and thought how much he loved them. His brother Phil sat beside Marilyn. Rich gave him a long look.

He had no notes with him—no fifteen pages of heavily prepared text. He just took a deep breath and began:

"Mr. Superintendent, faculty members, ladies and gentlemen, graduating class:

"Some twenty years ago I had a dream for this little valley. I dreamed of a great timber industry putting hundreds of people to work and bringing prosperity to everyone within reach of this area. I put everything I had into that dream. And it payed off. With your help we created an industry, a city, progress and prosperity. Hard work pays off.

"Until last week, I thought the result we had was exactly what it ought to be: Our prosperity in exchange for our hard work. We had worked the land and it had paid us big dividends—a town, a factory, good schools, nice houses. I was wrong."

He paused. His listeners rustled in their chairs. "Last night I had another dream. It was very different from the first one. In fact it was more like a nightmare.

"For the first time, I saw what we exchange for our progress. I saw fields become deserts from overgrazing and overfarming. I saw oceans die from overfishing. And I saw forests become lunar landscapes from overcutting. And I knew then that every bit of what we use from this planet has its price.

"I dreamed I stood out in space and looked on this planet as the astronauts had." He paused as the memory tightened his throat.

"Seeing the planet from that distance reminded me of the first time I saw my wife Marilyn hold our daughter Kim in her arms.

"I don't think I knew what love was until that moment. I felt the same when our son Dan was born. But last night, when I saw this priceless, irreplaceable planet hanging in the blackness of space, so alone, so ... *giving*, I felt that same intense love and protectiveness again. But now that love is overshadowed by fear.

"Would I have done to my children what I have done to this Earth? Would I have treated them with the disrespect and indifference that I have done to this valley? These forests?

"And yet—as if it were my divine right—that is exactly what I have done to this planet, and consequently to my children's future. "To your future," he said and gestured to the graduating class.

"This is what I have learned.

"First: If we have no ecosystem, we have no economic system. What is good for the planet is good for business. What is good for business must also be good for the planet.

"We who are in business must be the leaders to protect this planet because we are the ones who pursue and use its resources. We must use the same hard-driving instincts to reverse the breakdown of the ecosystems as we have used to create it. My motto has always been 'Hard work pays off.' In fact before last night, that was the essence of my speech. I stand by that, but I'd like to update it. 'Hard work—within the ecosystem—pays off.' There's no way we can ignore the cost of our demands on the environment and expect hard work to have more than a short-term payoff.

"You know what we have here in the timber industry? In this town, in this state? Dinosaur jobs. That's right. Dinosaur jobs. We're all going to be obsolete in less than ten years the way we're going.

"We've always been willing to go for a dollar's worth of jobs today at the cost of the ecosystem rather than take the time to create renewable jobs for tomorrow. The jobs will last when we factor in the cost to the ecosystem and renew it as we work.

"So, the choice is easy, isn't it? Dinosaur jobs or renewable jobs. Which do you want?" He paused to let that point sink in.

"Second: When we do well by the planet we do well by us all. One time, during a school tour through our plant, a fifth grader asked me if trees went to heaven when they died. I had never thought about it. 'Did trees have souls?' he was asking. I now feel that they do—as do all other living creatures. No more can we pretend that we humans are the only ones with wants and needs to be satisfied. We all do. We are all one soul, one life.

"My brother Phil told me two days ago that trees are not just board feet of lumber. I see that now. They are the pillars of the community in which they live. They give us breath and warmth and food and shelter, if not life itself. They connect earth to heaven and each of Earth's creatures to one another in community. Without them, every creature around them is without anchor, disconnected and diminished, unprotected and imperiled—including ourselves."

He thought of his moments as a red uakari jiving in the forest with his fellow creatures. He wished he could share the insights he'd gained but his audience would surely think he'd gone crazy. He'd tell Phil, though. Phil would love it. Marilyn would, too.

"Third: Let it not be said we knew what we had to do and did nothing. Those of us here tonight who are parents and grandparents of this graduating class, take heed. If we look forward to these fine young people perpetuating our families—having babies, raising them as we have, we need to change our ways.

"Plenty of alarming stories have appeared in the press about the state of our planet Earth. Still we've acted deaf and blind. It's time we faced the truth head on and adjusted our values and life styles accordingly so that we leave behind a decent world for our grandchildren to live in.

"We can't continue to subsidize the timber industry with taxpayers' money and let the Forest Service be our nursemaid. As long as we do that we sell logs to the Japanese at a foolishly low cost. We're too lazy to do even preliminary milling to add value to them. *They* are stockpiling *our* logs like money in *their bank*. Meanwhile, we're using inferior wood for our own products and shutting down mills because we can't afford to compete.

"We gave away our marketshare in the automobile industry in the '70s; we did the same with electronics in the '80s. Are we going to give away our position in timber in the '90s? How dumb can we be?

"When the dust settles, we'll be a nation of VCR's and no timber. Perhaps we will have balanced the trade deficit, but the trade off is entirely too costly.

"Are we as a nation so blind we won't quit until we have stripped this continent of every valuable resource? Do you and I really have the heart to hand a raped and pillaged land over to these young people? I have to believe we are smarter than that. Right now, we're acting just like a third-world country—selling off our natural resources for quick gain, letting other countries make them into high-priced goods. We'll eventually buy them back at high prices or end up being contract labor."

He took a deep breath and looked at Kim. Her face was filled with wonder. For a moment their eyes locked on each other, then he moved on.

"Finally, there is a Cree Indian legend that goes like this: 'When the Earth is sick and the animals disappear, there will come a tribe of peoples from all creeds, colors and cultures who believe in deeds, not words and who will restore the Earth to its former beauty. This tribe will be called the Warriors of the Rainbow.'

"Last night I met a Rainbow Warrior—beautiful beyond words. Guided by that warrior, I saw the world through new eyes. I saw everything I've just shared with you and much more besides.

"I had originally planned to urge you graduating seniors to follow my model and go forth to do business as it had been done for generations. I now urge you to do me one better. Make it your generation who sets the new tone for business. I challenge each of you to join that tribe of Rainbow Warriors.

"I intend to practice what I have just preached. Calvin Coolidge once said, 'The business of America is business.' I would amend that to say, 'The business of America—and every nation—is to lead the world in *eco*nomics.' From now on, the short-and long-term costs to the ecosystem must be factored in, however bitter it makes the bottom line at the moment. Remember, the choice is dinosaur jobs or renewable jobs."

Richard Lawless paused for a moment to survey his enraptured audience. The words he would say next would change his life forever.

"Though I am not as colorful as the one I met last night, you now see standing before you a Rainbow Warrior. I invite you to join with me to create a new Eden for you, your children, and your children's children."

In the split second following, he heard a cry of "All right, Rich!" He looked in Phil's direction. His brother was on his feet, clapping. In a moment so was the entire audience.

Rich felt tears in his eyes—tears of joy and relief. Already he could feel his eagerness to lead in this new challenge.

* * * * *

Richard Lawless sat at his desk the next morning, still feeling elated, somewhat confused and maybe a little smug. He had slept like a stone. That alone felt good, but the speech had been dynamite. Phil was ecstatic. Dan bounced around like a puppet. Kim squealed with pride and Marilyn and he had hugged like lovers. *That* had felt good.

On impulse he had asked Marilyn to drive up to the national forest with him next week. When she had agreed, he realized he'd have to cancel a meeting he'd called. Well, it was about time he put something other than business first.

The crowd had loved the Rainbow Warrior idea. The superintendent of schools wanted to talk to him about it. The principal had pumped his hand until he winced. "Become a Rainbow Warrior! What an idea!"

Well, Rich had said he'd become one. Now what? Where to begin? The meeting with the eco-freaks . . . he corrected himself—Planet Before People was in less than two hours. Obviously, he'd drop his plans to sue them for interrupting his business. Was it, at last, time to go beyond the letter of the law and get into the spirit of it? Instead of the minimum, do the maximum? Obviously so.

That meant rethinking, retooling, retraining—not just his place, but the Forest Service and the entire timber industry. . . .

A knock on the door interrupted his thoughts. "Yes?"

"Mr. Lawless, may I come in?" A tall, willowy woman with brown hair stood firmly in the doorway.

"Sylvia? Hello. What are you doing . . . uh, certainly. Come in." Rich rose from his chair and ushered her to a seat.

"Mr. Lawless, I spent the last two evenings calling over seventy people who work in this plant. Twenty three of them said they had child-care problems of one kind or another and thought an on-site day care facility would be one of the most helpful benefits anyone could give them.

"Here are their names and the ages of their children." She held out the paper firmly to Rich. He noticed that it trembled and suddenly respected her for this act of bravery.

He looked into her serious face and dark, determined eyes for a moment, seeing a flash of another penetrating face in his memory. So this was not just about trees. It was about people, too. They were all part of his ecosystem. Taking care of one meant taking care of the other.

Then he took the paper slowly from her hand, realizing that as he did so, he would be taking his first step as a Rainbow Warrior.

Part IV

Becoming a Rainbow Warrior

Are you ready to become a Rainbow Warrior? If you are, the place to begin is with personal conviction: You would rather be part of the solution than part of the problem.

The next step is education. Until you become informed you will not make intelligent choices and take appropriate action. Destruction of the Earth's rain forests is just one of the many problems we face. Nor is this destruction limited to the Pacific Northwest and Brazil.

- The island of Madagascar off the coast of East Africa has lost 90% of its forests.

- The Indonesian rain forests are seriously depleted.

- Australia's remaining rain forests, covering only 5% of their land mass, are protected by a small percentage of national parks.

- We are losing the lungs of the world.

Not only are we losing our lungs, but our ability to regenerate such vital parts. Along with that vital link

to the planet's health, we lose the wildlife and plants
that make up that community, we lose the soil which
pollutes our streams and rivers. What we create are
deserts.

To help you understand the environmental impera-
tives we now face, the Foresight Institute staff have
reviewed a number of excellent books for your use.
Knowledge breeds understanding, then the power to
act.

On the following pages you will find resources to
help you begin your journey as a Rainbow Warrior. We
invite you to pause a moment over these titles. Choose
a beginning point for educating yourself on the world
in which we live. Considering the pressures we as
humans place on this planet, where can you start to
make changes?

The first section is a bibliography of the best new
books available on the environment. When I went to
the library in August of 1988 to answer the question,
"What can I do to save the Earth?", hardly a single
recent book was available on the environment. Except
for the Worldwatch Institute's *State of the World Report*,
which recites chilling statistics about falling grain capac-
ities and environmental refugees, most copyrights were
1972 or earlier.

After Earth Day 1970, a brief spate of books appeared. Ralph Nader wrote about the wood pulp
industry; a few hardy souls spoke out about western
water rights; most of us slumbered. Somehow we
assumed environmental problems had all been solved
with Earth Day and the formation of the Environmental Protection Agency.

Then Earth herself woke us with a clarion call to
action and a whole new, wonderful set of authors
appeared to take up the cause.

To prepare this list the Foresight Institute staff reviewed every book whose publisher made available a copy. To those listed we give our Seal of Approval. A number of the titles are available through the Foresight Institute.

Following the bibliography is a list of associations and some financial tools you may want to participate in to strengthen your stand for a renewed Earth. Above all, do something. A century ago Edmund Burke, an Englishman, gave this brave statement. "No one makes the greater mistake than the one who does nothing because he thinks he can do so little."

To update that, in the slums of Manila, grandmother and community activist Angeles Serrano recently said: "Act, act, act. You can't just watch."

Part V

Your Environmental Bookshelf

The Foresight Institute's Seal of Approval goes to the books reviewed here. We regret this is a partial list. Space does not permit the listing of every new book and the omission of one in no way suggests its lack of merit. We have organized them into various sections for your convenience.

As we researched the available books, certain authors appeared again and again. Names like Rachel Carson—long after her death, David Attenborough, Gerald and Lee Durrell, Paul Ehrlich, cropped up on more than one book cover. These people courageously forged ahead while the rest of us turned indifferent backs to the environmental movement during the 1980's. They presented television specials, gave lectures, traveled and documented, as well as authored books. Their works are a testimony to elegant prose, fine photography as well as great reporting.

For general information, the GAIA books are hard to beat. (Gaia is the Greek word for mother Earth.) Published by Doubleday in London, the three books are the result of tremendous effort and cooperation from some of the finest scientific and political minds in the world. The three books that make up this set serve as an encyclopedia of environmental issues presented with stunning photographs and imaginative graphics. They are a *must read* for anyone starting out in environmental issues.

General Information

- *Gaia: An Atlas of Planet Management*, Dr. Norman Meyer, editor, foreword by Gerald Durrell. This book has no equal as an atlas and fount of information on the state of the planet. Published in 1985 it analyzes the health of planet Earth in seven critical areas: Land, Oceans, Elements, Evolution, Humankind, Civilization, and Management of the planet's resources. It offers insights into the causes of these environmental crises, full-color, highly imaginative drawings to bring dry statistics to life, as well as stunning photographs and numerous success and horror stories. The beginning text for Rainbow Warriors. Anchor Press Book, Doubleday Publishers, 8½ x 11", quality paperback binding, 270 pp, $18.95.

- *State of the Ark: An Atlas of Conservation in Action*, Lee Durrell, foreword by Gerald Durrell. This husband-and-wife-team manage the Jersey Wildlife Trust in Great Britain which has been instrumental in saving endangered species and reintroducing them into their natural habitats. This close look at animal and plant species and the impact of humans on them is crucial to understanding our place in our own ecosystem, planet Earth. The book offers sobering looks at man's thoughtless exploitation of fellow creatures and what those actions mean to our future. The same beautiful integration of text, full-color graphics and photographs makes this book easy to read and a pleasant way to get information. Doubleday Publishers, 1986, 8½ x 11", quality paperback binding, 222 pp, $14.95.

* *The Gaia Peace Atlas: Survival into the Third Millennium,* Frank Barnaby, foreword by Javier Pérez de Cuéllar, Secretary-General to the United Nations. The third part of the trilogy examines the underlying causes and motives for peace or war, the effects on the world economy of the military machines, the crises in nuclear and environmental terms. It offers strategies for short-and long-term solutions to redirecting the limited resources of a small planet toward sustaining peace and therefore life. Information is offered with the same flair for graphically creating impact for important points. Most illustrations are in black, red and white. Doubleday,1988, 8½ x 11", hardback, 270 pp, $29.95.

* *The Living Planet: A Portrait of the Earth,* David Attenborough. This book looks exclusively at the strange and exotic plant and animal life on Earth. Full of four-color, unusual photographs of such creatures as the large-eared, tiny Sahara fox, flying lizards, hibernating Monarch butterflies, it educates while delighting the reader. More a celebration of life on earth than an environmental text as such, it teaches care and respect through appreciation of the infinitely varied and fragile life systems with which we share resources. David Attenborough, described as the *Errol Flynn of zoology* is a British television producer who has devoted years to creating this volume as well as the equally popular, *Life on Earth.* Little, Brown, 1984, 7 x 10", quality paperback, 317 pp, $17.95.

All these titles are available through the Foresight Institute. See back page for ordering.

Plants and Animals

- *Save the Birds,* Roger Antony W. Diamond, et. al., sponsored by the Audubon Alliance. The most complete book you'll see on the world's bird population presents touching, incredibly beautiful photos and drawings of every kind of rare and exotic bird. The text details the loss of habitat, the *incidental taking* by hunters, ocean-net fishing and oil spills. A statement on the book cover says that a contribution from book proceeds will be made to the International "Save the Birds" account to help protect these species. Like the canaries in the mine shafts, these creatures signal our own imminent demise as they succumb to the poisoning and bruising of their ecosystems. A PRO NATUR book, Houghton Mifflin Company, 1989, 8½ x 11", hardback, 384 pp, $39.95.

- *The Greenpeace Book of Antarctica: A New View of the Seventh Continent,* John May, Foreword by Sir Peter Scott. Perhaps the first book on Antarctica that offers accessible information in the form of breath-taking photos, fine drawings, satellite pictures and charts and graphs. This is a handsome text written by an environmental writer who offers both the natural and scientific details that interest a lay reader. As the last continent on Earth becomes more heavily traveled and exploited, this book captures the beauty and importance of what is happening there. Doubleday, 1989, 8½ x 11", hardback, 190 pp, $24.95.

- *North American Wildlife: An Illustrated Guide to 2,000 Plants and Animals,* Reader's Digest Association. This is an encyclopedia of over 2,000 species, each depicted in full color with identifying information, plus range maps, habitat symbols and guide to ecosystems. Every living thing from wild peppermint to mayflies to humpback whales has its place in this volume. A hard-to-beat guide for students, teachers, scoutmasters, nature enthusiasts or anyone with an interest in fellow creatures. Color coded and extensively indexed. Reader's Digest Association, 1982, hardback, 550 pp, $22.95.

- *The New Dinosaurs: An Alternative Evolution,* Dougal Dixon, foreword by Desmond Morris, author of *The Naked Ape.* While this isn't an environmental book, it explores the impact of environmental events on the history of this planet. Dixon asks what if the dinosaurs had never become extinct? What if they'd lived on and evolved into present day forms? What would they look like? Then he invents with great detail and equal humor today's dinosaurs that live in place of elephants and giraffes and wolves. How about the whulk? The sprintosaur? The gimp, lank, footle, pangaloon, numbskull and watergulp? Dixon stays so well within the bounds of biological possibility that these animals could be real. Described as *nothing short of riotous,* it is a feast of dinosaur alternatives. If you like dinosaurs, you'll love these might-have-beens. Full-color drawings, descriptions, maps, glossary and index. Fawcett Columbine, 1989, 8½ x 11", quality paperback, 120 pp, $14.95.

Forests and Parks

- *Secrets of the Old Growth Forest*, David Kelly and Gary Braasch. It's about time someone produced a book about our own slender arc of rain and old-growth forest clinging to the northwest coast from Alaska to California. With minimal text and superb photos the book shows the treasures of the old-growth forests in Canada and the U.S.— the habitat of the spotted owl, the Pacific giant salamander and the pine martin. The secrets of life the authors expose in this forest are rare and perishing. An important statement about our own natural resources. Not every exotic creature lives in Brazil. Peregrine Smith Books, 1988, 8½ x 11", quality paperback, 100 pp. $15.95.

- *The Fate of the Forest: Developers, Destroyers and Defenders of the Amazon,* Susanna Hecht and Alexander Cockburn. Two fine investigative writers— Hecht who has spent a good deal of time in the Amazon, and Cockburn, described as a *radical writer*—have developed a detailed history of the Amazon region. The book explores the history of exploitation of the area from the time of its discovery to the present moment. They cover every subject from mining to cattle-grazing to exploitation of the native population and offer an extensive bibliography and index. An important information source for students of the Amazon region. Verso, 1989, 7 x 10", hardback, 266 pp.

- *Indonesian Eden: Aceh's Rainforest*, Michael Griffiths, forward by Emil Salim, Minister of State, Republic of Indonesia. We sometimes forget the rain forests of the South Seas. Here is a beautiful work to remind us of the wonders of yet another fragment of rain forest, this time in Sumatra. When will you ever see a mouse deer? Huge fruit bats? Orangutans and tigers at ease in their lairs? Both text and photos by the author show his intimate understanding of this area he has been photographing since 1986. Louisiana State University Press, 1990, 13 x 10", hardback, 111 pp, $24.95.

• *Shading Our Cities: A Resource Guide for Urban and Community Forests*, edited by Gary Moll & Sara Ebenrek, American Forestry Association. Articles from numerous experts on urban forests suggest the value of trees in a city setting. This is an informational source and action guide for both concerned citizens and interested professionals. Now that we truly appreciate trees for the lungs, air conditioners and natural filters that they are, we can take action for more trees along city streets and parkways. Island Press, 1989, 6 x 9", quality paperback, 332 pp, $19.95.

• *Our National Parks: America's Spectacular Wilderness Heritage*, Reader's Digest Association. A handsome presentation of America's treasured parks, this book covers sites from Maine to Alaska, from Wyoming to Florida. Beginning with the formation of Yellowstone in 1871, the authors trace the development of the national park system the best way possible—with vivid text and photos, maps and lists of features. This volumes captures the grandeur and beauty of these remaining jewels of natural wilderness in both close-up and panoramic perspective. Reader's Digest Association, 1989, 8½ x 11", hardback, 350 pp, $26.95.

Poverty and Overpopulation

If this topic seems out of place in an environmental list, then it's time to realize that both poverty and overpopulation have a direct impact on the environment. A degraded environment breeds poverty and vice versa. The new buzzword in environmental circles is *sustainable*. Too many people make our agricultural outputs, our water use, fossil fuel use, and our timber use *unsustainable*.

* *The Population Explosion,* Paul and Ann Ehrlich. Paul Ehrlich is author of *The Population Bomb,* published in 1968. In that book he sounded the alarm of the effects of overpopulation on the Earth's ability to sustain such life. In 1968 the population was 3.5 billion. Now it is 5.3 billion and rising at a rate of 95 million per year. We heard the message and failed to act. Now the *time for action is due, and past due.* Overpopulation is quite simply the cause of every environmental problem we experience today—from too much garbage to too much air pollution. The book warns that countries such as United States cannot point fingers at overpopulated countries such as India. The average citizen in the U.S. consumes more energy and creates more garbage than a dozen of his third-world counterparts. The authors' prescription may not be palatable but the growing problem is lethal. Anyone who cares about the quality of life on this planet in 50 years should read this book. These distinguished authors have won numerous awards for their research and stand on population issues. Both are associated with Stanford University. Simon and Schuster, 1990, 6 x 9", hardback, $18.95.

- *Ending Hunger: An Idea Whose Time Has Come,* The Hunger Project. A heart-wrenching appraisal of the difference between the haves and the have-nots. A relentless and beautiful photographic essay comparing grain piles in the United States to starving faces in Ethiopia. Text and graphs help to explain the problem of population, hunger and the distribution of wealth in the world. The Hunger Project, established in 1977, has gained close to four million supporters around the world to end hunger by the end of the century. Unfortunately, hunger is still an uphill fight and now that sustainable agriculture is threatened by environmental collapse, the reversal of hunger seems more distant than ever. This is a thorough and thoughtful approach to a difficult subject. It does not picture gaunt faces and emaciated limbs, but real people in real places—living, in some cases struggling against unendurable circumstances. Full page, color photographs, graphs, charts, glossary, extensive index and bibliography. Praeger Special Studies, 1985, 8½ x 11", quality paperback, 450 pp, $19.95.

Specialized Reference Sources

- *Blueprint for the Environment: A Plan for Federal Action,* edited by T. Allan Comp. A fascinating approach to the little-known world of federal laws and statutes available to exert changes for the environment. In 1987 a *Blueprint Steering Committee* made up of members of some eighteen environmental groups gathered. Their mission was to create more than 750 detailed recommendations for the federal government to address environmental problems. That accomplished, these were presented to

President-elect Bush at a breakfast meeting on November 30, 1988. They have since been put into the hands of most of the country's lawmakers. The format is simple. Most are half-page recommendations. Within existing departments, and usually with existing funds, the group recommends tighter use of the laws already on the books, better accounting systems, better enforcement of laws, formation of committees to oversee processes. The table of contents reads like the President's cabinet: For instance, Department of Agriculture—actions for wetlands, forests and timber, rivers and fisheries, pesticide prevention. Fascinating reading, an education in the intricacies, redundancies and inefficiencies of the U.S. government, and a must for citizen activists. Howe Brothers, 1989, 6 x 9", quality paperback, 335 pp, $13.95.

• *Economics As If the Earth Really Mattered: A Catalyst Guide to Socially Conscious Investing,* Susan Meeker-Lowry. Based on the idea that we need to return to the earth that which we take from it in good measure, the author has outlined a number of financial tools for doing so. She covers consumer boycotts, shareholder action, investments, loan funds, clearinghouses for hazardous wastes, community land trusts and much more. This extensive reference book deserves room on every Rainbow Warrior's bookshelf. New Society Publishers, 1988, 6 x 9", quality paperback, 282 pp, $14.95.

• *State of the World Report: A Worldwatch Institute Report on Progress Toward a Sustainable Society,* Lester Brown, et. al. Call the Worldwatch Institute the conscience of a sustainable society. The first *State of the World Report* appeared in 1984. Since then the popularity has grown as understanding has increased. This is now one of the most sought-after environmental reports, reportedly read avidly by business leaders and politicians the world over. It has been translated into all major languages. Each edition offers a report on different problems from hunger to energy consumption to transportation to AIDS. Although the facts it reports are frightening, each volume ends on a hopeful—if not quite optimistic—note. The book has been selected to accompany *Race to Save the Planet,* a thirteen-unit telecourse and ten-part public television series premiering in the fall of 1990. W.W. Norton Company, 1990, 6 x 9", quality paperback, 253 pp, $9.95.

* *Natural Resources for the 21st Century,* edited by R. Neil Sampson and Dwight Hair, American Forestry Association. The book is composed of papers presented at a conference on *Natural Resources for the 21st Century.* Held in Washington, D.C., in November of 1988, it reported on the condition of renewable resources in this country from wetlands to timber to wildlife. The volume closes with a declaration of interdependence. Island Press, 1990, 6 x 9", quality paperback, 350 pp, $19.95.

* *World Resources, 188-89 An Assessment of The Resource Base that Supports the Global Economy,* World Resources Institute and The International Institute for Environment and Development. An indispensable guide for finding levels of world resources. First published in 1986, this yearbook has grown in reputation and circulation. Now published in English, Chinese, Arabic and Spanish it offers new insights to the issues of natural resources and the environment. The volume analyzes an enormous

amount of information on conditions and trends in
global natural resources and the environment.
Graphs, charts, plentiful footnotes, regional focuses.
Basic Books, 1988, 8½ x 11", quality paperback, 372,
pp, $16.95. Although this yearbook is now out of
print, The Foresight Institute will offer the new
edition as soon as it is available.

Ecophilosophy

* *Deep Ecology: Living As If Nature Mattered,* Bill
  Devall and George Sessions. A thoughtful and
  thorough approach to the philosophical, psychologi-
  cal and sociological roots of today's environmental
  movement. For the first time poetry, philosophy,
  ecological insight and awareness of ourselves as
  fellow creatures is woven together in a narrative
  that is both moving and uplifting. Call it ecophilos-
  ophy. To read *Deep Ecology* is to experience *aha*
  after *aha.* It's like seeing yourself in a new mirror
  that stretches your inner rather than outer form. A
  touchstone for serious environmental students. The
  authors are long-time environmentalists and instruc-
  tors in California colleges. *Simple in Means, Rich in
  Ends,* by Devall is a second volume worthy of atten-
  tion. Peregrine Smith, 1985, 6 x 9", quality paperback, 266 pp, $11.95.

* *The End of Nature,* Bill McKibben. This book is less
  philosophy than alarm bell, but as an essay—absent
  are graphs, lists, directives—it fits more here than
  anywhere. McKibben looks at the methodical, pre-
  meditated cornering and killing of the natural world
  in flowing prose. This is an internal journey of
  another kind, examining our part in nature's death.

Wrapped in personal observation and experience, it is a gently but deeply confrontational look at the *either-or* choice we're making every day—either our material life as it now is, or a *biocentric* life. Nature will either become appreciated and protected for its own sake, or it will pass away. Like a son standing at the deathbed of his mother, the author poignantly looks at optional paths: Can she be saved? How? What heroic measures will it take? Or am I deluding myself? Should I just let her go? This book pierces the shallow concerns of our present lip service to the environment and knocks on the door of your heart. Read it and step into deep ecology. There will be no stepping back. Random House, 1989, 6 x 9", index, hardback, 215 pp, $19.95.

Citizen Guides

The return of Earth Day in April, 1990, brought forth the best from a dozen publishing houses at once. Not only was this a publishing phenomenon in itself, they each independently created a new kind of book: the *user-friendly* environmental book—scientific information and statistics presented to an unschooled audience. Some have succeeded at that formula better than others. We reviewed all those whose publishers made a copy available to us.

- *50 Simple Things You Can Do to Save the Earth,* The Earth Works Group. Certainly the first by a month and probably the most successful for reading ease and grasp of statistics. One- and two-page formats lay out truly simple, *I-can-make-a-difference!*, actions. Humorous titles help keep the information palatable to the most entrenched consumer of the throw-away society. Earth Works Press, 1989, 5½ x 8", quality paperback, recycled paper, 96 pp, $4.95.

*   *EarthRight: Every Citizen's Guide*, H. Patricia Hynes. Five environmental problems are thoughtfully addressed: Pesticides, solid waste, contaminated drinking water, depletion of the ozone layer and global warming. All subjects include a comprehensive, non-technical explanation of the causes and effects of the problem. The author includes a series of actions people can take and offers resources for further information. Individuals who are taking action in their community are profiled. An index and contents make looking for a particular subject easy. Author Hynes is an environmental engineer and professor of Urban Studies and Planning at MIT. Prima Publishing, 1990, 7½ x 9¼", quality paperback, recycled paper, 236 pp, $12.95.

*   *How to Make the World a Better Place: A Guide to Doing Good*, Jeffrey Hollender. The founder of Seventh Generation, a mail-order catalog of environmentally safe products, Hollender provides over 120 good ideas on how to effect positive social change. Covered in six chapters, each includes an introduction and several actions to take, including sources for more information. This book covers not only environmental issues, but banking and investing with a conscience, being a socially responsible consumer with credit cards, insurance, business, television, computers and more. Each action is designed to make the biggest difference in the least amount of time. Printed on recycled paper. Quill, William Morrow, 1990, 6 x 9", quality paperback, 302 pp, $9.95.

- *Our Earth, Ourselves: The Action-oriented Guide to Help You Protect and Preserve Our Environment,* Ruth Caplan, Executive Director, and staff of Environmental Action. This book covers global warming, ozone hole, air pollution, toxins, landfills, radioactive waste and proliferation, a global look at problems, environmental activism. A two-page layout in each chapter focuses on people making a difference. Many worthwhile lists of cities that exceed air-quality indexes, nuclear power plants in the United States, nuclear waste sites, companies with the highest toxic emissions, to name a few. Compiled by leading experts this hands-on guide provides concrete, practical advice on how to take up the cause for environmental change. Bantam, 1990, 6 x 9", recycled paper, quality paperback, 340 pp, $10.95.

- *Save Our Planet: 750 Everyday Ways You Can Help Clean Up the Earth,* Diane MacEachern. Dotted with cartoon drawings, this book helps the reader through various typical life situations: Your home, garden, garage, supermarket, school, office, community, apartment. The information is geared to help take action that will make a substantial impact on the world without making an appreciable difference in your way of life. The book designers made this information friendly with two columns on a page, lots of boxes, bullets, headings and so on to break up the text. *Bright Ideas* dot the pages, giving short, interesting action steps to put to use. Dell, 1990, 6 x 9", recycled paper, quality paperback, 210 pp, $9.95.

Good Reading

- *The Edge of the Sea,* Rachel Carson. Once a classic, always a classic. Though this was written in 1955, the subject of the buffer zone between the land and the deep sea is more significant now than ever. Waste on our beaches, repeated oil spills, loss of species along the shore, have all degraded this fertile strip we depend on for food and recreation. To read Rachel Carson's book is to hear the sound of the surf in the background, such is the power of her prose. This story of the surf life is expanded with fine pencil sketches of sea life by Robert Hines. Carson's most significant book was *Silent Spring* which warned us of the dangers of pesticides, namely DDT, and was instrumental in that pesticide being removed from the market. *The Edge of the Sea* is not so much a warning as a celebration, but in the context of today's threatened oceans and beaches, it becomes a siren to warn us to treasure this resource before we lose it. Houghton Mifflin, 1983, 6 x 9", quality paperback, 270 pp, $9.95.

- *Rush to Burn: Solving America's Garbage Crisis?* Newsday. Reporters from Newsday, a daily newspaper on Long Island, were first to locate the barge full of garbage that went begging for five months for a home for its unsavory load. That was 1987. Since then the newspaper has studiously explored and reported the problem of solid waste. The results of that investigation are presented here. Newsday won the Worth Bingham Award, the Page One Award for Crusading Journalism and the New York State Associated Press Award for In-Depth Reporting for their study of this issue. They call incineration the riskiest form of garbage disposal. Island Press, 6 x 9", quality paperback, recycled paper, 270 pp, $14.95.

- *Ozone Crisis: The 15-Year Evolution of a Sudden Global Emergency,* Sharon Roan. Almost a scientific who-dun-it as the author narrates the scientific world's discovery of the hole in the ozone layer. From 1975 to the present, the track of action and inaction on the ultimately deadly loss of ozone is traced. The story gives a good understanding of the politics involved in creating change. The author's lively journalistic prose keeps the story interesting as she weaves in scientific fact with a human story of society's disinterest in coming to its senses and making needed changes. A journal approach based on a detailed time line of events. A good read as well as an excellent resource for research. Bibliography and index. Wiley & Sons, 1989, 6 x 9", hardback, 270 pp, $18.95.

- *The Quiet Crisis and the Next Generation,* Stewart Udall. Udall was Secretary of the Interior for both the Kennedy and the Johnson administration. *The Quiet Crisis* was first published in 1963 with a foreword by John F. Kennedy. The book traces the values we as Americans have placed on land and our relationship to it from Thomas Jefferson onward. In this 25th anniversary edition, Udall has added to the history important chapters—those heroes who have stepped forward to champion the Earth in the years since. This is a book packed with information and stories of heroic action in the face of danger or indifference. The forward by John Kennedy stands, a memory of a simpler era and a timeless statement to a new generation. Extensive time line and index.

Peregrine Smith Books, 6 x 9", hardback, 298 pp, $18.95.

The Environmental Home

This list will grow as more authors put their experiences in print. Here are three sources that cover some basic information.

- *The Nontoxic Home: Protecting Yourself and Your Family from Everyday Toxins and Health Hazards,* Debra Lynn Dadd. This book covers just about every question you might have on protecting yourself from foreign and unsafe chemicals, additives, gases, etc. It gives safe alternatives to chemically-created beauty and hygiene products, plastics, food additives, cleaning products, how to minimize the dangers of second-hand smoke, video-display terminals and other environmental poisons. The author attributes such health problems as headaches, depression, sterility, cancer, birth defects and genetic changes to our poisonous home and work surroundings. Parents of young children should certainly be informed of these innocent-looking dangers around the home. Dadd experienced such health problems herself until she researched alternative ways to clean, cook, clothe and care for herself and family and cured herself of chronic illness. Index divided into Products, Hazards, and Health Effects. Dadd is also the author of *Nontoxic and Natural* and publisher of *Everything Natural* newsletter. Jeremy Tarcher, 1986, 5½ x 8¼", quality paperback, $9.95.

- *The Smart Kitchen: How to Design a Comfortable, Safe, Energy-Efficient, and Environment-Friendly*

Workspace, David Goldbeck. This book revolutionizes kitchen design as it incorporates recycling, composting and other environment-friendly ideas into everyone's favorite room. Any of us already recycling are faced with piling up our own garbage until we can dispose of it. Golbeck spent a year relieving us all of experiencing *landfill-in-the-kitchen* syndrome. He has created an in-counter composting chute, an outside pickup, shelf and draw space for newspapers, paper bags, aluminum cans and all the other packaging problems we struggle with as our consciousness grows. A large part of the book includes energy efficiency in the kitchen. He takes on the refrigerator—a major burner of electricity, the dishwasher, the range and other appliances and tells how to make them more efficient. Many ink drawings, maintenance troubleshooting checklist, resource list for every kind of product or design help needed, extensive bibliography and index make this book a bargain in the time it takes off your learning curve. Author also publishes *True Food Newsletter* and is co-author of four other books on food. Ceres Press, 1989, 8½ x 11", quality paperback, $15.95.

• *Recipes for a Small Planet,* Ellen Buchman Ewald. Although there are other books on vegetarian cooking and recipes, none perhaps is as enduring as this one. Published in 1973, it has been steadily popular since. Not too many books do that well. It is not just a cookbook with chapters of fine recipes, but an instruction book to a meatless alternative. Every recipe is defined by approximate grams of usable protein and percent of average daily protein needed. The title is a take-off from a book by Frances Moore Lappé, *Diet for a Small Planet,* which argues that we *eat lower on the food chain,* a suggestion now back in vogue. Here is a book that not only tells how but why. It follows the principles of natural food cooking and eating and also contains charts to obtain high-quality, complete protein by the right combinations of legumes, grains, seeds and dairy products. Yes, greens and grains, folks. Step right up. If you'd like to enter the environmentally sound world by eating, here's a book that will tell you how. Glossary of foods, index. Ballantine, 5½ x 8", plastic comb binding, 366 pp, 7.95.

Children's Bookshelf

Not only will the next generation be given tough choices but the task of building new life styles. Here are some outstanding books that will help them get in touch with natural values—a place to start.

- *Environmental Starters,* Gould League of Victoria, Australia. We found these two books in Australia in the summer of 1989. We have found nothing to match them yet. Where do you start to educate young children to understand their ecosystem? This book gives you everything from *Environmental Bingo* to *Rubbings* to *Lichen Looks,* to *Pebble Puzzles.* Colored and line drawings, hand printed, easy text make the book friendly and attractive. All game pages can be photocopied for quick use. All games and experiences have been tested over many years of use. If you have young children (ages 4-7) or teach them, this book is a treasure. With a little imagination many of these experiences can be adapted to teens and adults. Gould League of Victoria, Australia, 12 x 8", quality paperback, 62 pp, $12.00.

- *Outdoor Environmental Games,* Gould League of Victoria, Australia. These games are for older children 7-12 and teach ecological principles. The games are designed as directed-play learning experiences and teach discovery, problem solving and some teaching of ecology. These games are concerned not just with information but in creating positive feelings and attitudes toward the environment. They develop a code of behavior towards the fragile Earth while they create an element of excitement. Oh, yes, they're also fun! Because the book is from Australia you get a couple of games called *Dingoes, Wallabies and Grasses* and *Wombat Squash.* They can be changed to *Deer and Antelope,* or use them as they are. This is an imaginative, inventive and practical book for a most-needed task. Attractive colored and black-and-white drawings and hand lettered text. Gould League of Victoria, Australia, 12 x 8", quality paperback, 64 pp, $12.00.

- *Sharing the Joy of Nature: Nature Activities for All Ages,* Joseph Cornell. This book is rich in insight and suggestions for approaches to nature learning and fun. It requires reading ahead of time so that you understand the four steps of *flow learning* and can apply them to your outings. You will be amply rewarded for the investment in reading time. A half dozen games and experiences lead you through each of the four stages of flow learning, then you can mix and match forever after. Much information for the group leader on both ecology and group dynamics, including a chapter on bringing out the best in others. Experiences teach the enchantment of nature, the joy of discovery, the playful spirit in learning, and stewardship and idealism. Line drawings, black-and-white photos, appendices. The author is a naturalist, educator and workshop leader in nature awareness around the globe. Dawn Publications, 1989, 6 x 9", 168 pp, $9.95.

- *Naturewatch: Exploring Nature with Your Children,* Adrienne Katz. A comprehensive activity book for older children. More than 50 experiences, many self-directed. How do you catch a spider's web intact? How do plants drink? Which insects depend on which plants for food? This book is packed with short recipes for discovering, nurturing, identifying, planting and protecting. A special section on nature crafts shows how to create seed jewelry, tie-dye art and more. The book contains over 200 black-and-white drawings. Take the book on summer vacation or on a trip around the block. Share it with your kids and share with them the wonder of the natural world. Addison-Wesley, 1986, 7½ x 8½", quality paperback, $7.95.

- *Happy Veggies,* Mayumi Oda. This is a beautifully-illustrated, read-aloud book for toddlers. It's not about how good they taste, but how they grow, sing, dangle, hide, feast and dream. Illustrated by an internationally acclaimed artist whose Matisse-like paintings bring a new dimension to pedestrian veggies, this book is a song of joy and praise that little ones will find entrancing. Parallax Press, 7½ x 10½", hardback, 34 pp, $12.50.

- *A Carabou Alphabet,* written and illustrated by Mary Beth Owen. A lovely, rhymed recital of the life of the carabou from Antlers to Zero weather. Full-color illustrations wrapped around each letter of the alphabet teach a great deal about North America's own reindeer, an animal we know little about. Having been hunted to extinction in Northern United States, they are now being reintroduced in some areas through programs like the Maine Caribou Transplant Project. A portion of proceeds of the book go to support that project. This is a book for all ages – even adults – who want to learn more about one of nature's elegant creatures. Includes glossary of reindeer and Arctic-life terms. The Dog Ear Press, 12 x 9", hardback, 34 pp, $14.95.

Associations You Can Join

These organizations are just a few of those that can help you save the tropical forests as well as endangered species. If you are interested in an organization not listed here, ask your reference librarian for a directory of associations.

Center for Environmental Education
   624 9th St., NW
   Washington, D.C. 20001

Environmental Defense Fund
   1616 P. St., NW, Suite 150
   Washington, D.C. 20036

Greenpeace Rainforest Campaign
   P.O. Box 3720
   Washington, D.C. 20090-6099

Rainforest Action Network
   300 Broadway, Suite 28
   San Francisco, CA 94133

Rainforest Alliance
    295 Madison Avenue, Suite 1804
    New York, NY 10017

Sierra Club
    Information Services
    730 Polk Street
    San Francisco, CA 94009

Tropical Forests Project
    World Resources Institute
    1735 New York Avenue, NW
    Washington, D.C. 20006

Wildlife Conservation International
    c/o New York Zoological Society
    Bronx, NY 10460

World Wildlife Fund/Conservation Foundation
    1250 24th Street, NW
    Washington, DC 20037

Financial Tools

A new tool of the many now at work for the environment is specific to the rainforest-preservation cause. Working Assets Long Distance has been created among groups like Greenpeace, Environmental Defense Fund, and the Rainforest Action Network *and* US Sprint. When you use US Sprint for a long distance call, 1% of your charges go to these and other non-profit groups to protect endangered species. And—as they say in their advertising—perhaps even to protect our own.

Working Assets Long Distance
230 California St.
San Francisco, CA 94111
1-800-877-2100

For more complete information read *Economics as if the Earth Really Mattered*, by Susan Meeker-Lowery and *How to Make the World a Better Place,* Jeffrey Hollender. These authors list every type of financial involvement from mutual funds to credit cards sponsored by the World Wildlife Fund to health and home insurance.

Details of these books are described in the bibliography of *Call of the Rainbow Warrior.*

The Foresight Institute

If you have progressed to this point, perhaps you're ready for a step into real commitment. Here is information about The Foresight Institute.

The mission of the Institute is to heal the Earth through publications, training and awards. This is what the Institute offers:

- *User-friendly* environmental books, such as *Call of the Rainbow Warrior, Earthcare: Eight Actions to Lead Your Community in Environmental Change,* by Twyla Dell due out in late 1990, and other titles by other authors.

- The Environmental Bookshelf, some of the selections of which we reviewed on the previous pages, to schools, organizations and corporations. Large organizations may wish to donate the Environmental Bookshelf to local schools and colleges.

- The Environmental Leadership Program to cities throughout the nation to create a positive change in local and regional areas.

Specifically, the Institute serves as a catalyst in the environmental movement. We invite 100 persons at a time in a community to experience the Environmental

Leadership Program. We create a space for those civic and business leaders, educators, and concerned citizens to examine past and current issues, actions taken and not taken, prices we may have to pay if we do not change, and what actions we can take to make a difference in our future.

The Foresight Environmental Leadership Program is a two-weekend retreat in a rustic setting. Weekend one concentrates on the problem of environmental loss. The week between offers participants an opportunity to examine their world from a new perspective, focus on local issues, and gather information. Weekend two focuses on solutions and creates a space for participants to come to a commitment about creating environmental change in their community.

The Foresight Institute does not advocate violent or subversive action, but rather encourages volunteer, entrepreneurial, consumer, political, and educational activities to create needed change. The Institute provides information, networking and moral support for these leaders to fulfill their goals.

Graduates in the ELP training network receive a newsletter, attend quarterly meetings, and may qualify for awards for their achievements. They become part of the Foresight Directory and mentors to the next crop of participants, locally or nationally.

For further information, please contact:

The Foresight Institute
10108 Hemlock Drive
Post Office Box 13267
Overland Park, KS 66212
913-383-3359

Give the Gift of Becoming a
"Rainbow Warrior"
to Your Friends, Family, and Colleagues!

**Remember! Every book ordered from us,
helps plant a tree.**

YES, I want to become a Rainbow Warrior! Please send the following titles from the Environmental Bookshelf so I can get started.

Qty	Title	Price	Total
_____	*Call of the Rainbow Warrior*	$12.95	_____
_____	_____	_____	_____
_____	_____	_____	_____
_____	_____	_____	_____
_____	_____	_____	_____
_____	_____	_____	_____
_____	_____	_____	_____
_____	_____	_____	_____
_____	_____	_____	_____
_____	_____	_____	_____
_____	_____	_____	_____
_____	_____	_____	_____
_____	_____	_____	_____
_____	_____	_____	_____
_____	_____	_____	_____

Sub-total	_____
Kansas Sales Tax	_____
Shipping & Handling	_____
TOTAL	_____

(over)

(Kansas residents please include 5.75% sales tax.) Canadian orders must be accompanied by a Postal Money Order in U.S. funds. Allow 30 days for delivery. Add $2 shipping per book. *Order five books and pay by check—we'll pay the shipping!*

☐ Check/MO enclosed • Charge my ☐ VISA ☐ MC

Name _____

Phone _____

Address _____

City/State/Zip _____

Card # _____

Expires _____

Signature _____

**Check your leading bookstore
or
Call your credit card order to
(913) 383-3359**

Please make your check payable and return to:

**F☺RE
SIGHT
INSTITUTE**

10108 Hemlock Drive
Overland Park, KS 66212